21st Century Skills Library

REAL WORLD SCIENCE

PROTECTING ECOSYSTEMS

Leanne Currie-McGhee

Cherry Lake Publishing
Ann Arbor, Michigan

CHERRY LAKE Publishing

Published in the United States of America by Cherry Lake Publishing
Ann Arbor, Michigan
www.cherrylakepublishing.com

Content Adviser: Laura Graceffa, middle school science teacher; BA degree in science, Vassar College; MA degrees in science and education, Brown University

Photo Credits: Cover and page 1, © newphotoservice/Shutterstock; page 4, © Anton Gorlin/Shutterstock; page 6, James May/Alamy; page 8, Trevor Payne/Alamy; page 9, © Shutterstock; page 10, © Torsten Lorenz/Shutterstock; page 11, © Hope Alexis Milan/Shutterstock; page 13, AP Photo/Elaine Kurtenback; page 15, Morley Read/Alamy; page 16, Alaska Stock LLC/Alamy; page 18, © hvoya/Shutterstock; page 20, © Steve Noakes/Shutterstock; page 22, © Joseph Gareri/Shutterstock; page 23, AP Photo/Al Grillo; page 24, Mike Dobel/Alamy; page 27, AP Photo/M. Spencer Green

Library of Congress Cataloging-in-Publication Data

Currie-McGhee, L. K. (Leanne K.)
Protecting ecosystems / Leanne Currie-McGhee.
  p. cm.—(Real world science)
Includes index.
ISBN-13: 978-1-60279-462-7
ISBN-10: 1-60279-462-6
1. Nature conservation—Juvenile literature. I. Title. II. Series.

QH76.C86 2009
333.95'16—dc22   2008040808

Cherry Lake Publishing would like to acknowledge the work of
The Partnership for 21st Century Skills.
Please visit www.21stcenturyskills.org for more information.

TABLE OF CONTENTS

CHAPTER ONE
Natural Changes in Ecosystems   4

CHAPTER TWO
Changes Caused by People   10

CHAPTER THREE
Wise Use of Ecosystems   16

CHAPTER FOUR
Restoring Damaged Ecosystems   23

Real World Science Challenge Answers   29

Glossary   30

For More Information   31

Index   32

About the Author   32

NATURAL CHANGES IN ECOSYSTEMS

Too much or too little rain can cause changes in an ecosystem.

Ecosystems are made up of plants, animals, and their surroundings.

All parts of an ecosystem work together. A change to one part can affect

all the others.

Ecosystems are always changing. Many changes occur naturally. Weather,

for instance, may bring changes to an ecosystem. A very rainy year might cause

more plants to grow. A very dry year might lead to fewer or smaller plants.

Natural changes are neither good nor bad. They are a fact of life in all ecosystems. Sometimes these changes result in a healthier ecosystem. In a healthy ecosystem, all parts are in balance. The plants get enough sunlight and water. The animals get enough food. Sometimes natural changes throw an ecosystem out of balance. This is when there is too little or too much of something. If there is not enough sun, plants may die. Without enough plants, animals may die. If most of the plants and animals die, the ecosystem collapses.

REAL WORLD SCIENCE CHALLENGE

Plants are affected by changes in temperature, rainfall, and sunlight. To find out how changes in sunlight affect plants, fill three pots with potting soil. (Make sure each pot has small holes in the bottom for drainage.) Plant one tomato plant in each pot. Label each pot, one through three. Allow the plants to get the following amounts of light per day:

Number 1: No light

Number 2: 6 hours

Number 3: Continuous light

Give each plant equal amounts of water for ten days. Keep the soil moist, but not soaked. For ten days, record the growth of each plant. What did you find?

(Turn to page 29 for the answer)

Lava flows down a volcano in Guatemala, wiping out plants and animals in its path.

The results of natural changes can be seen over different periods of

time. Some of these results can be seen right away. When Chile's Chaitén

volcano erupted in 2008, the volcano wiped out plants and animals for

miles around. The results of the volcano's erupting were easy to see. At

other times the results of natural changes take years to show up. When a

volcano erupts, for instance, it might drop a layer of ash on the land. After thousands of years, the ash creates very rich soil where all kinds of plants can once again grow. This type of change is known as geologic change.

Landslides are also a form of geologic change. In 2007, there was a major landslide in New Zealand's Mount Aspiring National Park. Hundreds of thousands of tons of rock smashed into a river on the valley floor. This created a dam 230 feet (70 m) high. The water backed up and made a lake that is 1.2 miles (2 km) long and 1,640 feet (500 m) wide.

Ecosystems can change for other reasons, too. If a small lake fills up with sand, gravel, or other

In 2004, a huge tsunami struck in the Indian Ocean. It was caused by a powerful underwater earthquake. The force of the quake created massive waves. By the time the waves reached land, they were about 100 feet (33 m) high. Thousands of people were trapped by the tsunami and killed. It also damaged ecosystems. It washed silt into the ocean. The silt smothered coral reefs, an important type of undersea ecosystem. On shore, the tsunami tore down mangrove forests and palm trees. It washed out beaches. Sea turtles' and other animals' habitats were destroyed. Thousands of these animals died. Scientists think it could take decades for these ecosystems to recover.

A tree that once grew on a river bank now stands in the middle of a New Zealand lake.

types of sediment, plants that lived in the lake will die. After a long while,

other plants such as grasses may take their place. This type of change is

called succession. It can occur with both plants and animals.

Extreme weather can also bring changes to ecosystems. In just one

day, Hurricane Katrina caused major changes to forests in the southern

United States. Most of the forests were in Mississippi. The hurricane knocked down the oak, hickory, and pine trees.

Chinese tallow trees and Japanese grass grew up in place of the trees. These are

Hurricane Katrina stripped leaves from trees in Mississippi.

invasive species. Invasive species are plants and animals that are not native to an area. They invade an area after a major change.

The tallow tree's sap can kill insects, birds, and small animals. Many animals left the forests after the tallow trees came. The forests are now filled with many invasive plants. There are few native animals and plants.

Some changes threaten an ecosystem's balance. Other changes keep it balanced. One thing is always certain. There will always be change.

CHAPTER TWO

CHANGES CAUSED BY PEOPLE

Fish are the main food source for more than one-fifth of the world's people.

We humans depend on many types of ecosystems. We drink water from natural springs and lakes. We fish in oceans for food. We take trees from forests to build houses. We depend on all of these ecosystems, but we are not always careful with them. Some of our actions have hurt ecosystems and the many creatures that depend on them.

Fish is the main food source for more than 1 billion of the world's people. Fishing companies catch fish to help feed people. They caught 95 million tons (86 million tonnes) of fish in 2005. This is almost five times what they caught in 1950.

The world's oceans once had plenty of fish. Now some parts of the oceans are overfished. This means fish are caught at a rate faster than they can reproduce. Scientists warn that the world may run out of fish for people to eat by 2048.

Waste from factories and farms pollutes water, killing plants and fish.

Overfishing does not just threaten an important food source for people. It also hurts ocean ecosystems. Without fish, there is more algae, bacteria, and jellyfish. Too many of these species can kill coral reefs. Off the coast of the Caribbean island of Jamaica, algae and bacteria have smothered coral reefs.

People have also harmed rivers and lakes. Fertilizer from farms flows into streams. Sewage runs into lakes. Factory waste spills into rivers. Nearly 40 percent of American rivers and lakes are too polluted for fishing or swimming.

REAL WORLD SCIENCE CHALLENGE

To learn how water pollution changes as it moves downstream, fill a cup, a 1 liter or 1 quart jar, and a 4 liter or 1 gallon jug with water. Add and stir two drops of red food coloring to the water in the cup. Pour all but a small amount of water from the cup into the jar. Pour all but a small amount of water from the jar into the jug. Put a lid on the jug and shake. Observe the colors in each container. What happens?

(Turn to page 29 for the answer)

A couple fishes in a Chinese lake. Pollution may prevent this in the future.

Other countries have created problems like this, too. The largest

inland freshwater lake in China is Bagrax Lake. People use it for drinking

water. They may not be able to for much longer. Each year more than

487 million tons (442 million tonnes) of pollution runs into the lake.

This includes fertilizer from farms and wastewater from households and

companies. The pollution has made the lake water salty and undrinkable.

21st Century Content

Around the world, people use palm oil. They used 153 million tons (139 million tonnes) in 2007. Palm oil comes from palm trees. Its main use is as cooking oil. Palm oil companies cut down the rain forest's trees and plants to grow palm trees for oil. Without native trees and plants, rain forest animals do not have places to live or food to eat. Some animals move to other parts of the rain forests. There may not be enough food for them. They starve and die. Many palm oil plantations are in Malaysia. Malaysian orangutans have lost much of their habitat. The orangutan population has decreased by 10 percent since 2004. Ecologists warn that their numbers will continue to decrease unless changes are made.

The salt has also harmed birds, including ducks and geese. They cannot drink the salty water. The birds either die or leave the area to find freshwater.

Tropical **rain forests** provide another example of an ecosystem hurt by human actions. Experts think that 50 million acres (20 million ha) of rain forests are destroyed every year. One reason they are being destroyed is for oil.

There are oil deposits in rain forests. People use the oil for energy. Oil companies cut down trees and plants to clear areas for drilling. They build pipelines to transport oil. These pipelines

Workers clean up after an oil spill in the Amazon rain forest.

sometimes break. Oil spills into the rain forests. The oil pollutes water.

Experts estimate that the rain forests lose 137 plant, animal, and insect

species every day. This is because these creatures lose their homes and food

when the rain forests are cleared and the oil pollutes their water supply.

The world's ecosystems are in danger. This threatens the health of

people, other animals, plants, and the planet as a whole.

CHAPTER THREE

WISE USE OF ECOSYSTEMS

Concerns about overfishing in Alaska have led to many laws.

Mitch Keplinger makes money from the ocean. He also takes care of the ocean. Keplinger knows that he must use the ocean responsibly to preserve it. This is true for all ecosystems.

Keplinger is a fishing boat captain. He fishes near Alaska's Kodiak Island. He follows that state's fishing rules. The rules say how many fish can be caught in a season. The rules limit fishing boat sizes. They also limit net sizes. Keplinger thinks these are good rules. The rules save

fish populations. This in turn protects ocean plants and other

ocean animals that depend on fish. Fishing by these rules is called

sustainable fishing.

REAL WORLD SCIENCE CHALLENGE

People like to live and play near rivers and streams. They build houses, buildings, golf courses, and roads near rivers and streams. However, these can cause soil erosion. Soil erosion is when dirt and silt are pushed down toward rivers and streams. When it rains, the soil washes into these waterways. The soil fills up the rock crevices that are in the water. The rock crevices are home to crayfish, snails, mussels, and insects. With their homes destroyed, these creatures die. Can you think of ways to prevent soil erosion caused by development?

(Turn to page 29 for the answer)

Some people catch and sell fish to make money. Others sell trees

from rain forests. Many poor people live in rain forests. They chop

down the trees and sell the lumber. Taking trees hurts the rain forest.

There are other products people can take from the rain forest without harming it. And they can still earn money to live on.

Cashew nuts can be harvested without cutting down rain forest trees.

One product is the cashew nut. The cashew nut grows on trees in the Amazon rain forest. Villagers can pick cashew nuts without cutting down the trees. They sell the nuts to companies like Ben & Jerry's. Ben & Jerry's makes Rainforest Crunch ice cream with cashew nuts from the Amazon rain forest. In 2006, Brazil produced and sold 236,140 tons (214, 223 tonnes) of cashew nuts.

In central and southern Africa there are many savannas. Savannas are large areas of grasslands with shrubs. Elephants, rhinos, lions, and giraffes live in savannas. Some Africans hunt elephants to sell their tusks for ivory. Others hunt rhinos to sell their horns. When these animals are killed, it affects the ecosystem. For example, the elephants remove the savanna's trees to eat their bark. If the trees were not removed, the grasslands would become forest. Then grass-eating animals, like antelopes, would not have food.

Some African governments have found new ways for people to earn money from the savannas.

21st Century Content

Rain forest plants can be used to make medicines. These plants grow back at a quick rate so this is a wise use of rain forests. One-fourth of Western drugs are made from rain forest ingredients. For example, a type of periwinkle flower grows in Madagascar's rain forests. It can be made into medicine. It makes a drug that has helped increase the chance of surviving childhood leukemia. It also makes a drug that is used to treat Hodgkin's disease, a type of cancer. More research of rain forest plants could lead to many more medicines. Less than 1 percent of the rain forest trees and plants have been tested to see what medicines they could produce.

Elephants can be seen in African savannas that have been turned into national parks.

South Africa has turned many of its savannas into national parks. There are more than 20 national parks in South Africa. Tourists can pay money to visit the parks. Tourists can watch, but not hurt, the lands, plants, and animals.

Villagers cannot hunt or farm in the parks. However, villagers can sell crafts and other items to tourists. The South African government pays some villages for their land. They paid South African money equaling almost a half million

U.S. dollars to the Makuleke village. The government uses the village's land as part of Kruger National Park.

Wetlands are getting some help, too. Wetlands are areas where the land is wet and muddy. Three-quarters of wetlands are privately owned. People use them for farms or to build houses on. In the United States, the Clean Water Act makes sure people use the wetlands wisely.

For example, companies can build factories near wetlands. But the factories must limit their pollution. They cannot pollute the wetlands with their waste. Companies that do not follow the Clean Water Act must pay a fine.

21st Century Content

The Marine Stewardship Council (MSC) is a worldwide nonprofit organization. Its mission is to promote sustainable fishing. Fish caught in a sustainable way get an "MSC" label. People can buy "MSC" fish at places like Wal-Mart and Whole Foods stores. People buy fish with this label to help keep the oceans healthy. Enough fish are left in the sea to reproduce. This keeps the ocean balanced. Without fish, algae, bacteria, and jellyfish reproduce at great rates. Too many of these species can kill coral reefs.

Laws protect wetlands like this one from factory pollution.

Ecosystems can be used and protected at the same time. People need to

find more ways to wisely use ecosystems. This will keep ecosystems healthy

for a long time.

CHAPTER FOUR

RESTORING DAMAGED ECOSYSTEMS

Reef balls are lowered into the waters near Whittier, Alaska.

People around the world now know that healthy ecosystems matter. And they are taking steps to restore the damage done to some of them.

Todd Barber grew up in the Cayman Islands. He is a scuba diver. He has seen damaged coral reefs all around the islands.

Pollution harmed the coral reefs. Barber is helping to undo the damage.

Barber and his father found a way to restore coral reefs. They came up with the reef ball. The reef ball is a ball of concrete. It is six feet high and six feet wide (1.8 × 1.8 m). It is hollow inside. The reef ball's rough surface has holes in it. The surface and holes attract corals, algae, and sponges. They settle on the ball and a reef grows. More than 500,000 reef balls have been placed in over 59 countries. Coral and fish are thriving in the areas where reef balls have been placed.

Reforestation is another way to restore ecosystems. People can restore damaged forests. To do so, they plant new trees and plants. They give the area fresh soil. This is taking place in forests all over the world.

Spruce and fir seedlings in Idaho will be planted in reforested areas.

It is being done in old mining areas throughout Ohio. There, forests were destroyed by decades of coal mining. What was once the Jockey Hollow East Mine is now a state wildlife area; 55 acres (22 ha) have been restored to forestland. The soil was replaced: 33,000 hardwoods, including oak, chestnut, and sycamore trees, were planted. Plants were also added. Now the forest ecosystem has been restored.

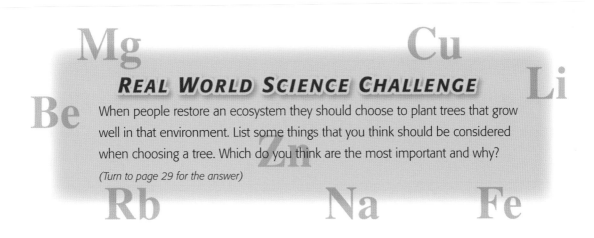

REAL WORLD SCIENCE CHALLENGE

When people restore an ecosystem they should choose to plant trees that grow well in that environment. List some things that you think should be considered when choosing a tree. Which do you think are the most important and why?
(Turn to page 29 for the answer)

While trees are needed to restore forests, water is needed to restore wetlands. Around the world many wetlands have been drained. The water

In 2008, the Boy Scouts helped restore forests and wetlands. They completed the ArrowCorps5 project. Five thousand Boy Scouts worked on five restoration projects at U.S. parks. They did this in five weeks. At some sites they got rid of invasive species. At other sites, they removed trash. At the Bridger-Teton forest in western Wyoming, the scouts repaired trails and removed unused fences. The fences kept the forest's elk from freely moving around the forest. More than 1,000 Boy Scouts and leaders worked at this site.

was drained so people could use the land to farm.

These wetlands can be refilled with water. One way is to block or fill in ditches that were dug to drain the wetlands.

People plant native plants after the wetlands get water. The plants and water bring back animals and birds. Then the ecosystem is restored.

An old cranberry farm is being restored to a wetland in New Jersey. The New Jersey Conservation Foundation is restoring 1,100 acres (440 ha) of the farm. The foundation is plugging canals. This will keep water from flowing out of the wetland. People are planting native trees and plants.

River ecosystems are also being restored. People are cleaning up the Anacostia River in Washington, D.C. For years, raw sewage flowed into the river during major storms. The storm water caused the sewage pipes to overflow. Sewage ran into

Green roofs like this one in Chicago can help save resources.

the river. The storm water also flushed trash from the streets into the river.

This is changing. The city is putting green roofs on buildings. Green roofs are roofs that are covered with plants and grass. The green roofs absorb

Learning & Innovation Skills

Emil Viola gets paid to restore wetlands. Construction companies pay him thousands of dollars for every acre (0.4 ha) he restores. Some construction companies destroy wetlands when they build houses and buildings. By law, they must then restore an acre somewhere else. Companies pay Viola to do this for them. Viola bought more than 5,000 acres (2,000 ha) of farmland and forest in Virginia and North Carolina. He turns them into wetlands. He fills in ditches that drain water from the wetlands. This allows water to stay on the land. He plants native plants and trees in the area. The Environmental Protection Agency checks to make sure that his work meets wetland standards. His company has made at least $14 million helping restore wetlands.

storm water. Less storm water gets into the sewer pipes. Then less sewage overflows from the pipes. This reduces the sewage that goes into the river. Also, less trash from the streets flows into the river. The river's water is cleaner than it was ten years ago. There is also more aquatic life in the river.

People have learned that they can repair ecosystems. If everyone gets involved, more ecosystems will be restored. That is good for the ecosystems. It is good for the animals, plants, and people who depend on them.

REAL WORLD SCIENCE CHALLENGE ANSWERS

Chapter One

Page 5

Each plant should have grown to a different height. Plant number one should have grown the least. Plant number three should have grown the most. This shows how a change in weather can affect the rest of the ecosystem. If a forest gets fewer sunny days than normally, the plants get less sunlight. Then the plants will not grow as much. This will affect the rest of the ecosystem. Plant-eating animals will have less food and could die or leave the forest.

Chapter Two

Page 12

The water should be deep red in the cup, pale red in the jar, and pink to nearly colorless in the jug. As the food coloring mixes with a larger amount of water, the color is harder to see. This is like what happens with water pollution. When waste is first dumped in a river, you can see it. As it flows downstream the waste is diluted. This means its strength is lessened. This is because the pollution mixes in with more water. After a while, the waste can barely be seen. However, it is still there polluting the river.

Chapter Three

Page 17

One way to protect the fish is to take care of the plant life on the shore. Plants' roots keep soil from going into the water. If the shore has been cleared of plant life, plant new plants. Use native trees, shrubs, wildflowers, and grasses with strong root systems. The roots will hold the soil in place.

Chapter Four

Page 25

When you choose a tree, you must pick one that will grow well in that environment. The most important things to consider are sun, soil, moisture, and temperature. This is because these are what most affect a tree's growth. Find out how much sun the area gets, what the soil is like, how much water the area gets, and what the average temperatures are. With this information, you can pick a suitable tree.

Glossary

ecosystem (EE-koh-sis-tem) a defined area made up of animals, plants, and their environment

green roof a building's roof that is covered with living plants and grass to help hold rainwater and decrease the storm water that flows into waterways

habitat (HAB-uh-tat) the area and environment where an animal or plant lives

native (NAY-tiv) originally living or growing in an area

rain forest (RAYN-for-est) a forest in an area that gets lots of rainfall

reforestation (ree-FOR-eh-STAY-shun) replacing soil and native trees and plants in damaged forests

savannas (sa-VAN-ahz) grasslands that contain scattered trees and hardy brush

succession (suck-SE-shun) the changing of plants and animals in an ecosystem over time

sustainable fishing (suh-STAYN-uh-buhl FISH-ing) fishing that leaves enough fish in the sea or river to allow fish populations to be restored naturally

FOR MORE INFORMATION

Books

Davis, Barbara. *Biomes and Ecosystems.* Strongsville,
OH: Gareth Stevens Publishing, 2007.

Pipe, Jim. *Earth's Ecosystems.* Strongsville,
OH: Gareth Stevens Publishing, 2008.

Web Sites

Environmental Protection Agency—EPA Student Center
www.epa.gov/region5/students/ecosystems.htm
U.S. government information about different ecosystems and ways to protect them

KidsSavingtheRainforest
www.kidssavingtherainforest.org/
Kids who are helping restore and protect rain forests

Natural Resources Defense Council—Make Waves
www.nrdc.org/makewaves/
Information on how to protect oceans

World Wildlife Fund—Freshwater Wetlands
www.panda.org/news_facts/education/middle_school/habitats/
freshwater_wetlands/index.cfm
Information about wetlands conservation

INDEX

Africa, 19–21
algae, 12
Anacostia River, 27–28
ArrowCorps5 project, 26

bacteria, 12
Bagrax Lake, 13
Boy Scouts, 26
Brazil, 18
Bridger-Teton forest, 26

cashew nuts, 18
Chaitén volcano, 6
changes
    human-caused, 10–15
    natural, 4–9
China, 13–14
Clean Water Act, 21
coal mining, 25
coral reefs, 7, 12, 21, 23–24

deforestation, 14–15

ecosystems
    changes in, 4–9
    composition of, 4
    impact of humans on,
        10–15
    restoring damaged, 23–28
    unbalanced, 5
    wise use of, 16–22
elephants, 19–20

fish, 11–12, 21
fishing, sustainable, 16–17, 21

geologic change, 7
green roofs, 27–28

habitat destruction, 7
humans, impact of on
    ecosystems, 10–15
Hurricane Katrina, 8–9

invasive species, 9, 26

Jamaica, 12
Jockey Hollow East Mine, 25

Kruger National Park, 21

lakes, 12–14
landslides, 7

Malaysia, 14
Marine Stewardship Council
    (MSC), 21
medicines, 19
Mount Aspiring National
    Park, 7

national parks, 20–21
native species, 9
natural changes, 4–9
New Jersey Conservation
    Foundation, 26

ocean ecosystems, 12
oil, 14–15
overfishing, 11–12

palm oil, 14
pollution, 12–14, 15,
    27–28

rain forests, 14–15, 17–19
Real World Science
    Challenge, 5, 12, 17, 25
reef balls, 24
reforestation, 24–25
regulations, 16–17
river ecosystems, 12, 27–28

savannas, 19–21
sewage, 27–28
South Africa, 20–21
storm water, 27–28
storms, 8–9
succession, 8
sustainable fishing, 16–17, 21

tallow trees, 9
tsunami, 7

volcanoes, 6–7

water pollution, 12–14, 15,
    27–28
weather, 4, 8–9
wetlands, 21, 25–26, 28

ABOUT THE AUTHOR

Leanne Currie-McGhee lives in Norfolk, Virginia, with her daughter, Grace, and husband, Keith. She has been writing for educational publishers for more than five years. Aside from writing, she enjoys tennis, scuba diving, travel, going to the beach, reading, and spending time with her family.